TOOLS FOR CAREGIVERS

- **ATOS:** 0.6
- **GRL:** C
- **WORD COUNT:** 40

- **CURRICULUM CONNECTIONS:**
  animals, habitats

Skills to Teach

- **HIGH-FREQUENCY WORDS:** a, and, are, here, in, is, it, mom, see, the, they, this, with
- **CONTENT WORDS:** away, baby, black, comes, foal, group, lion, lives, right, run, safe, stands, stripes, walks, white, zebra
- **PUNCTUATION:** exclamation points, periods
- **WORD STUDY:** long /a/, spelled ay (away); long /e/, spelled ee (see); long /o/, spelled oa (foal); multisyllable words (baby, zebra)
- **TEXT TYPE:** information report

Before Reading Activities

- Read the title and give a simple statement of the main idea.
- Have students "walk" though the book and talk about what they see in the pictures.
- Introduce new vocabulary by having students predict the first letter and locate the word in the text.
- Discuss any unfamiliar concepts that are in the text.

After Reading Activities

Zebra babies are called foals. Horse babies are also called foals. Explain to the readers that zebras and horses are part of the same family. This means that they share some traits. How are zebras and horses similar? How are they different? Make a list with the headings "similarities" and "differences." Write the readers' answers under each heading. Discuss their answers as a group.

Tadpole Books are published by Jump!, 5357 Penn Avenue South, Minneapolis, MN 55419, www.jumplibrary.com

Editor: Jenna Trnka **Designer:** Anna Peterson

Photo Credits: Justin Black/Shutterstock, cover; prapass/Shutterstock, 1; charissadescanderlotter/Shutterstock, 2–3, 16tl; Danita Delmont/Shutterstock, 4–5; Four Oaks/Shutterstock, 6–7, 16bl; caizier/Shutterstock, 8–9, 16br; 1001slide/iStock, 10–11, 16m; Scandium/Shutterstock, 12–13 (zebras); Anton_Ivanov/Shutterstock, 12–13 (lion), 16tr; milehightraveler/iStock, 14–15, 16bm.

Library of Congress Cataloging-in-Publication Data
Names: Nilsen, Genevieve, author.
Title: Zebra foals / by Genevieve Nilsen.
Description: Tadpole edition. | Minneapolis, MN : Jump!, Inc., (2019) | Series: Safari babies | Includes index.
Identifiers: LCCN 2018024757 (print) | LCCN 2018027526 (ebook) | ISBN 9781641282512 (ebook) | ISBN 9781641282499 (hardcover : alk. paper) | ISBN 9781641282505 (paperback)
Subjects: LCSH: Zebras—Infancy—Juvenile literature.
Classification: LCC QL737.U62 (ebook) | LCC QL737.U62 N55 2019 (print) | DDC 599.665/71392—dc23
LC record available at https://lccn.loc.gov/2018024757

ZEBRA FOALS

by Genevieve Nilsen

TABLE OF CONTENTS

tadpole books

ZEBRA FOALS

This is a foal.

foal

It is a baby zebra.

It stands right away.

mom

It walks with mom.

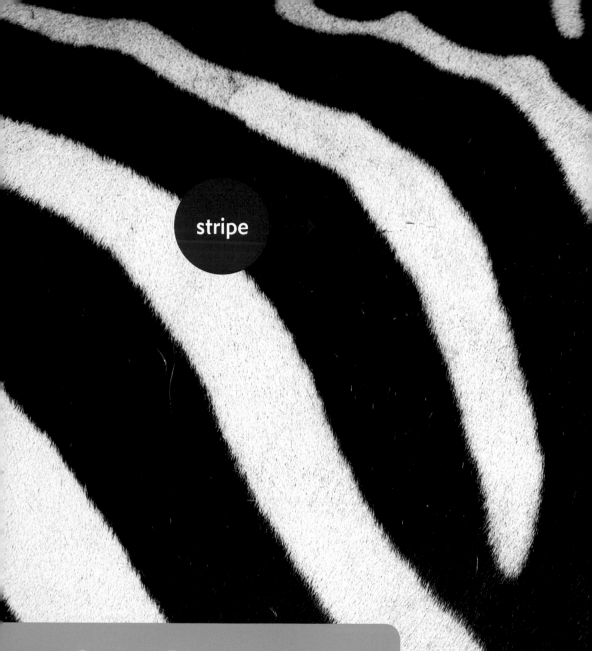

stripe

See the stripes.

They are black
and white.

It lives in a group.

lion

Here comes a lion!

Run!

They are safe.

WORDS TO KNOW

foal

group

lion

mom

safe

stripes

INDEX